DALASIA JACKSON

# From Bullet to Breakthrough

*A Memoir of Survival, Resilience, and Transformation*

*First edition*

ISBN: 979-8-218-87892-4

*This book is dedicated to:*

*Anyone facing the impossible, trapped by fear, pain, or uncertainty — may this story remind you that hope can survive even the darkest nights, strength can rise from brokenness, and a full, meaningful life is still within reach.*

# Contents

# Acknowledgments

To everyone who walked with me through the darkest and brightest parts of this journey — thank you.

To my parents and my family, who carried me with love, patience, and strength when I couldn't carry myself.

To the doctor who saved my life and the incredible nurses at Sparrow Hospital who fought for me every single day.

To the nurses, therapists, and staff at Mary Free Bed who pushed me, supported me, and helped me rebuild piece by piece.

And to every person who showed kindness, offered a prayer, lifted my spirit, or believed in my healing — your support shaped this story as much as I did.

This book exists because of all of you.

# From Bullet to Breakthrough

*A Memoir of Survival, Resilience, and Transformation*

# CHAPTER 1

---

# THE SHIFT

I didn't notice the gun first.

I noticed the shift in the room.

The energy changed — tense, heavy —
like the air itself was warning me.

I couldn't explain it, but something inside me said:
Something is about to happen.

Not fear.
Not imagination.
Discernment.

I glanced toward the door and saw him walk in.
Not surprised.
Not welcomed.
Just wrong.

My body reacted before my mind did.
A tight feeling moved through my chest — serious, focused,
alert.

My instinct whispered:

Leave.

But I stayed.

————

## THIS WASN'T HIS FIRST TIME.

What happened that night wasn't random.

Long before that moment —
before the gunshot that changed my life —
there were warnings.

His grudge had nothing to do with me.

In fact, we barely knew each other.

We'd seen each other in passing a handful of times.

He and a relative of mine had once been friends.
They ended up entangled in legal trouble a couple of years
prior.

Later, the court documents became public.

My family member posted them to social media.

That single act humiliated him.
His pride was bruised.
And he wanted retaliation.

Not with words.
With violence.

———

## THE FIRST SHOOTING

Late at night, while everyone in the house was asleep, he came.

We woke up to the aftermath —
bullet holes in the back of my mother's car.

We were confused.
Worried.
With no idea who did it or why.

———

## THE SECOND SHOOTING

He came again when the house was empty —
all of us away at a family event.

One bullet pierced my bedroom wall and went through my
bed.

3

Another traveled through a family member's room, into my
parents' room,
and exited through the back of the house.

Any one of us could have been standing in its path.

———

## THE THIRD SHOOTING

The last incident happened when my father was out of town.
Just me and my mother were home.

A little after midnight, gunshots shattered the quiet.
We woke up screaming — frantic, terrified, helpless.

We didn't know why this was happening.

We didn't know who to fear.

A week later, we began hearing whispers —
people saying he was bragging about what he had done all over town.

So when I saw him walk through the door on New Year's Eve,
when my chest tightened and instinct told me to leave,

it wasn't paranoia.

It was recognition.

————

That night there was no buildup.
No time to prepare.

A gunshot cracked through the room.

A burn tore through my body — hot, sharp, instant.

People screamed.
Chairs scraped across the floor.
Everyone ran in different directions.

The world around me was loud,
but inside my head — it was silent.

I prayed out loud.

"Lord God, please keep me alive.
Forgive me for every sin.
If you heal me, I will do anything."

My vision blurred.
My body felt heavy.

And just like that —
everything went dark.

————

## FLASHBACK — WHO I WAS BEFORE

Before that night, I wasn't the popular girl.
I wasn't the "nerd" either.

I was just me.

A black girl with style, personality, softness, and dreams.
I had friends — different circles — and I blended wherever I
wanted to be.

I wasn't the loud one.
I wasn't trying to be seen.
But people liked me.
People talked to me.
People knew my presence without me having to demand
attention.

Dance was a big part of my life.
It was my happy place —
my peace.

Dance was woven into every part of my life.
I danced at school.
I trained at a studio outside of school.
And on Sundays, I worshiped on the praise team at church.

Dance didn't define me.

But it expressed me.

My body spoke when my voice didn't feel like talking.

At sixteen, my plans were simple:

Graduate.
Dance.
Live a full life.

I thought I had time.

I thought I knew what the next chapter of my life would be.
I didn't know my entire world was about to shift because of
one gunshot.

# CHAPTER 2

---

## THE EVE OF CHANGE

The night before, I was filled with excitement.

Growing up, my parents were strict — structured, protective, and intentional.
I earned trust by keeping good grades and respecting their rules.
Even with that, the answer to parties was usually *no*.

New Year's Eve was no different.

When I asked to go, my mom didn't hesitate:

"No. You're not going."

Not because she didn't trust me —
but because she didn't trust the world,
especially at night,
especially around unpredictable people.

But I pushed back.

"I'm a good kid."
"My grades are perfect."
"I don't ask to go anywhere."
And my strongest argument:
"It's my sister's party — at her house."

To me, that made it safe.
Controlled.
Familiar.

I wasn't asking to go somewhere random.
I was asking to go somewhere where family was.

I begged with teenage persistence,
trying to prove I was responsible —
that I deserved this one night of freedom.

Eventually — against her better judgment — she gave in.

Not because she stopped worrying,
but because she didn't want me to feel isolated, different,
or restricted while everyone else my age was having fun.

Later that night, just before midnight, she called.

Her voice was calm but firm —
a warning wrapped in love.

"It's almost midnight. Stay away from windows.

People shoot guns in the air when the New Year hits.
And what goes up… must come down."

I promised her I'd be careful.

I had no idea those words weren't just caution.

They were prophecy —
a mother's instinct trying to protect me from something I
couldn't see.

———

After work — a full shift at Younkers Department store —
my mind wasn't on retail counters or hanger racks.
My mind was already at the party.

I had two outfits ready —
one cute and girly,
the other fly — Jordans and all.

I knew I was going to be cute.
I knew I was going to be fly.

My hair was braided, my lip gloss applied.
Everything was perfect.
Everything just right.

I was ready to celebrate,
to ring in the New Year,
to have fun with my family and close friends.

When we arrived, family and friends filled the living room and
kitchen.
People were laughing, talking, moving in circles.

But there was one friend — loud, belligerent, drunk —
who immediately caught my attention.
Something about him felt off.

He was just too loud.
Too exaggerated.
Too chaotic.

Then came the knock on the door.

The loud guy announced:
"My friend is here."

And just like that, the tension shifted.
The air thickened — heavy, almost pressing down on me.

I instinctively knew — this was a setup.

The loud friend immediately put his arm around him.
Both of them smirking — too confident, too familiar, too
calculated.

My stomach dropped.
Something inside me screamed, *This isn't right.*

Nothing about that moment felt casual.

The air shifted — heavy, tense —
like the room itself knew danger had entered.

My instinct whispered:

Leave.

Before I could react, a woman came in behind him —
very drunk, hostile, looking for a problem.

Her words were sharp, aggressive, and loud.
She wasn't there to celebrate.
She was on an assignment.

Voices raised.
Arguments flared.
Energy changed fast.

My sister yelled for everyone to get out,
trying to end the chaos before things escalated.

The shooter looked back at us —
and smirked.

Not a nervous smirk.
Not a friendly one.

A devious one.

Then he walked out the front door.

Seconds later — gunshots.

The house exploded into panic.

Everyone ran upstairs or toward the exit.
People were screaming.
Chairs scraped.
Doors slammed.

I was the last one moving — just me and one other guy left downstairs.

I ran up the steps behind the group.

And then it happened.

BOOM.

A burning heat shot through my back — instant, sharp, violent.

My body dropped.

A table broke part of my fall.

Another gunshot hit a light, and the room went black.
Just me and the other guy — crouched in a corner, knees to his chest, frozen.
Too scared to move.

I tried to speak.
Tried to stay calm.

"Can I use your phone?"

No response.
He just stared — shocked, unmoving.

Blood pooling internally.
Pain radiating.
Darkness swallowing the room.

I prayed out loud:

"Lord God, please keep me alive.
Forgive me for all my sins.
Please, Lord, if you heal me, I will do anything."

My voice wasn't a whisper.
It was desperate.
Raw.

He watched me pray — frozen, silent — as I stayed conscious.

Seconds later, footsteps pounded the stairs.

My sister's voice cut through the darkness — high, panicked,
cracking:

"My sister's shot! My sister's shot! Somebody call!"

Then my cousin's voice:

"I'm calling — I'm calling!"

My niece and nephew's father ran downstairs.

He tried to lift me, inspecting my back,
trying to see where the blood was coming from.

"You're not shot," he said —
because there was no blood pouring out.

But I felt it.

"Put me down.
Please — put me down,"
I begged through the pain.

He lowered me.

Then my cousin's brother and her father came through the
front door.
They lifted me the same way —
examining me,
trying to figure out how to help.

They were helpful, focused, trying to keep me calm.

"I can't... put me down," I cried,
my voice shaking.

And then —
she appeared.

My cousin's mother.

When she touched me,
it was different.

Warm. Comforting. Motherly.

She held my hand and leaned over me,
tears filling her eyes.

"I'm here, baby. I'm right here."

I remember her palm against my cheek —
a gentle, light slap — guiding me back to consciousness when I
started drifting.

"Stay with me, baby. Stay with me."

My breaths grew shallow.
My vision blurred at the edges.

And then — through the front window —

red and blue lights flashed.

Relief washed over me.

Thank God.

In that moment,
everything changed.

# CHAPTER 3

---

## THE RESCUE

The moment the doors opened, paramedics flooded into the
house.

A stretcher appeared beside me, and hands lifted me onto it.
Pain lit up every nerve in my back — sharp, burning,
undeniable.

"We're going to take off your shoes," one of them said.

I nodded, waiting to feel their hands.

Then I looked down…
My shoes were gone.
I hadn't felt them being taken off — but they were gone.

They began wheeling me outside.

Cold air rushed across my skin,
sirens echoing somewhere close,

voices everywhere.

As soon as we reached the yard, the scene hit me all at once:

Yellow police tape.
Blue and red lights bouncing across houses.
Crowds pressed together behind the tape, faces strained with panic.

Then I saw my brother.
He was pushing through people, full of anger and fear.

"That's my sister! That's my sister — LET ME THROUGH!"

Hearing his voice cracked something inside me.

"Mama!" I yelled.
"Mama!"

They loaded me into the ambulance.
The doors slammed.
Sirens screamed.

Inside, the paramedic leaned over me with trauma scissors.

"I'm cutting your clothes off now."

She narrated every step —
deliberate, calm, focused.

Fabric slid away.

Cold air hit my skin.
She began marking my body with a pen.

"Tell me everywhere you can feel," she said.

She started at my thighs.

"Here?"
"Yes, I feel that."

She moved lower.

"Here?"
"Yes."

She continued down, and when she reached below my knees, I couldn't feel anything.

The single word hung in the air — sharp and cold.

I swallowed hard, my voice shaking.
"Am I… paralyzed?"

She didn't rush.
She didn't lie.

"We don't know yet," she said softly.
"But you're alive. Stay with me."

The ambulance jerked and made a sharp turn.

"We're rerouting! Another hospital has the trauma team ready
— they're better equipped for her!"

My vision kept blurring. Each time it did, the paramedic
tapped my cheek lightly.

"Stay awake. Keep talking to me."

My mom's voice came through the chaos — not physically, but
in my mind.

*Stay away from windows... what goes up must come down.*

She didn't know how true those words would be that night.

And under all of it — the sirens, the pain, the fear —
all I kept thinking was: Don't let me die here.

When we reached the hospital, the back doors flew open.

They rushed me out, the stretcher hitting every bump on the
pavement.

The hallway was bright and freezing.

A nurse saw me being pushed in and shouted:

"Gunshot victim — ROOM 3, NOW!"

Everything happened at once —

Hands on my body.
Machines beeping.
Voices overlapping.

"Blood pressure dropping."
"IV ready."
"Move, move, move!"

I stared at the ceiling tiles passing above me,
feeling the world spin further and further away.

The last thing I remember was a voice close to my ear:

"You're safe now. We've got you."

Then everything faded.

While I was unconscious, my body was fighting for its life.

The bullet had caused massive internal bleeding.
Blood was filling spaces it shouldn't — quiet, hidden,
dangerous.

A clot formed.

It traveled toward my heart.

Machines began screaming, numbers dropping fast.

"Her blood pressure is crashing!"
"We're losing her!"

My parents weren't allowed in the room,
but they could hear the chaos through the walls.

Both of my parents prayed
with everything in them.

Then — a surgeon stepped forward.

Firm voice.
Steady hands.
No hesitation.

"I'm going to save your baby girl."

He ordered the team to place me into a medically induced
coma
so my body could survive the trauma long enough
for them to operate.

Machines took over.
My body went still.
The world continued without me.

And I slipped into darkness.

# CHAPTER 4

---

## WAKING UP

Light.

Too bright.
Too sharp.

I opened my eyes to a ceiling I didn't recognize,
in a room that didn't feel real.

I tried to speak.

Except—
I couldn't.

Something was lodged in my throat.
Thick. Heavy. Suffocating.

My body reacted instantly.
I tried to move, to signal what I needed,
but wires, tubes, and monitors held me down.

My mom rushed toward me.

"Baby — don't pull anything out!"

Her voice wasn't crying,
but it was pure panic.

She hovered over me, gently pushing my hands down,
her words fast and frantic:

"I know, baby. I know. Calm down — you're okay."

I wasn't trying to pull cords.

I was trying to tell her:

I need more pain medicine.

But I couldn't talk.
The tube silenced every word.

I motioned toward my mouth again,
pointing to my arm, frustrated,
trying to sign what I needed.

She repeated, still panicked:

"Stop, baby — don't pull the wires!"

Inside, I was screaming:
*I'm not pulling wires — HELP ME!*

24

Then I saw him.

My dad.

Calm.
Steady.
Focused.

I pointed to him urgently, motioning him closer.

He leaned in, studied my face,
looked at my hand gestures…

And instantly understood.

"You need more medication?" he asked.

I nodded — hard.

He turned to the nurse.
"She's asking for pain medicine. She needs more."

My mom's jaw dropped, like,
*How did you understand THAT?*

Even in that moment,
that tiny bit of comic relief broke through the trauma.

We still laugh about it to this day.

The nurse leaned over me,

25

her voice soft and steady.

"Sweetheart… you have a trach in. That's why you can't talk."

My chest heaved, my throat stung,
and I realized the weight of it:
being awake, aware, and unable to speak.

When I turned my head,
I saw both of my parents standing there.

Their faces were exhausted.
Relieved.
Anchoring me back to life.

I didn't know what tomorrow meant.
Or what my body would never do again.

But in that moment,
the only thing that mattered was:

I woke up.
And they were there.

# CHAPTER 5

---

## THE HEARTBREAKING NEWS

The trach had been removed days earlier,
and for the first time since everything happened,
the fog of medication was finally lifting.

I was awake.
Present.
Aware.

The room was dim, machines humming steadily,
my parents sitting nearby — exhausted,
their bodies in the chairs but their minds somewhere far away.

They whispered in low, tight voices.
I wasn't supposed to hear anything,
but one sentence cracked everything open:

"…movement in the legs…"

My heart stopped.

Movement?
Whose legs?
My legs?

When they turned away for just a moment,
I tested it.

I stared at my legs and told my brain:

Move.

Nothing.

I tried again — harder, desperate.

Still nothing.

My stomach dropped.

Before I could ask,
the doctor turned around.
He didn't sugarcoat it,
didn't build up to the point.

He just said:

"Right now, you're paralyzed from the waist down."

The words hit like a punch to the chest.

My mom covered her mouth.

Her eyes filled — trembling, terrified, broken for me.

I didn't breathe.
I didn't blink.

I was frozen in disbelief.

My voice shook as I whispered,
"Will I walk again?"

The doctor stepped closer, steady and honest.

"You have an incomplete spinal cord injury at L1. That means
there is a possibility. It could go either way.
It's a 50–50 chance."

Fifty–fifty.

A coin flip on the rest of my life.

Everything inside me cracked.

Tears came without warning —
hot and violent,
rolling down my cheeks faster than I could wipe them away.

The grief wasn't soft.
It wasn't quiet.

It was a scream trapped inside my body.

I sobbed until the crying turned into something else —
something louder,
something sharper.

Anger.

Anger at the world.

Anger at whatever had taken my legs.

And then, for a moment,
that anger shifted toward the only people in the room.

My parents.

They were the ones who signed the papers.
They were the ones who fought to keep me alive.

In that moment,
I wasn't thinking about love or gratitude.
I was thinking…

Why did you save me?
Why didn't you let me go?

I didn't hate them.
I was just drowning in pain
and looking for something — anything — to blame.

I stared at the ceiling and felt like
my body had betrayed me,

my future had vanished,
and everything I once imagined for my life
had been ripped away without warning.

They didn't say a word,
but the heartbreak on their faces told its own story.

In that moment,
I wasn't grieving the loss of movement.

I was grieving the loss of who I thought I would be.

## JOURNAL ENTRY — Letter to the Shooter (Age 16)

DATE: 2016

Dear P———,

Why?

What was the purpose?

You took so much from me.

Not only did you take my ability to walk, you also took my ability to dance.

You took away my self-esteem.

You took away my independence.

You almost took my life.

You made me this angry person that's full of hate

I hate you, and I hope you get everything that you deserve.

# CHAPTER 6

---

# LEARNING TO LIVE AGAIN

Before I even made it to Mary Free Bed, I hit a wall.

I stopped eating.

Food had no taste.
I had zero motivation.
Absolutely no energy.

They handed me a tiny one-pound weight, and I couldn't even lift it.

My arm shook uncontrollably, and I remember thinking:

How am I supposed to relearn life if I can't even lift this?

Every day, nurses tried to feed me, tried to encourage me, tried to get me involved in therapy — but I refused.

I was angry.

I was empty.
I was exhausted.

Eventually, the surgeon told me plainly:

"You cannot go to rehab if your body isn't strong enough to participate."

That was the first time I realized I could get stuck there forever if I didn't try.

So I forced myself to eat.

Little by little.
Sip by sip.
Bite by bite.

And slowly, strength returned to my body.

———

## DAMAGED DONE

The bullet didn't just enter my back —
it shattered it.

It fractured my spine and exploded into pieces on impact.
There were fragments everywhere.

To remove the remnants, surgeons had to open my abdomen —
cutting through the front of my body

to get to the back.

I woke up with staples, drains, tubes, and a thick back brace
that wrapped around my torso.
I wore that brace for months and months.

———

## SEEING MYSELF FOR THE FIRST TIME

My nurses would take me down a hallway with big windows so I
could look outside — just to get me out of the room for a
minute.

But one of those days, I caught my reflection in the glass.

For a second, I froze.

I looked so small.
So thin.
So… unfamiliar.

My body didn't look like mine anymore.

I felt disgusted.
Not at my scars —
but at how fragile and broken I looked.

I didn't want to see myself after that.
Didn't want mirrors.
Didn't want reflections.

I hated what I saw
because it reminded me of everything I had lost.

———

## THE FIRST THERAPY GOAL: SIT AT 90 DEGREES

One of my first therapy goals at the hospital was something
most people never think twice about:

Sitting.

Just sitting at 90 degrees.

The pain was unreal —
like fire ripping through my spine.

Every session, they would raise the bed slowly, inch by inch.

I screamed — loud.
Louder than I knew I could.
Pain that broke me open.

My dad was there during one of those sessions.

He stood at the foot of the bed,
his eyes filling with tears,
trying to be strong,
trying to hold it together.

When the screams became too much, he stepped in:

"That's enough. No more therapy today."

Not because he didn't want me to get better,
but because a father can only watch his child suffer so much.

———

## HOSPITALIZED FOR THREE MONTHS

When I finally gained enough strength, I was transferred to
Mary Free Bed Rehabilitation Hospital in Grand Rapids.

About an hour away from home.

Far enough that I couldn't see my family whenever I wanted.

No casual drop-ins.
No siblings stopping by.

Just weekends,
if schedules allowed.

That distance hurt.

But I wasn't totally alone.

My cousin — my favorite cousin, just a year younger — lived
in Grand Rapids and stayed with me.
With her, I didn't feel like a patient.
I felt like me.

And looking back, her support during that time meant more than she'll ever know. She kept me grounded when my world felt upside down.

———

## ANGER, HEALING, AND HUMILITY

The staff was incredible.

They were kind.
Patient.
Encouraging.

The hospital wasn't the problem.

I was.

I was pissed off at the world.

Therapists tried to help me relearn basic things:
how to sit up,
how to transfer,
how to balance.

It felt humiliating to be taught how to live inside a body I used to command.

———

## SECRET MISSIONS

My cousin figured out a way to break my anger.

We'd go on what we called missions.

We rolled down the halls,
peeked around corners like spies,
quietly pressed the elevator button.

We laughed,
we whispered,
we acted like we were breaking out of a top-secret government
lab.

For a moment,
I wasn't thinking about paralysis or rehab.

I was just a teenager
on a mission
with my best friend.

———

## FAMILY SUPPORT

My parents made that drive too.

My dad came whenever he could —
especially when staff called about me acting up.

He brought things to decorate my room:
• Flowers

- Family pictures
- Art supplies
- Puzzles and little activities

He did whatever he could to make the hospital feel less like a hospital and more like a bedroom.

My mom was there as well.
She showed up to support me, to encourage me, to remind me I wasn't forgotten.
Both of them were fighting the battle with me.

———

## MEDICATIONS

At one point, I was taking thirty medications at a time.

My mom organized them into containers,
making sure every pill, every dose, every time was right.
It was overwhelming, but it kept me alive. It kept me going.

———

## THE NIGHTS NO ONE SAW

But when visiting hours ended
and the lights dimmed…

The silence hit.

I cried.
A lot.

I prayed.
I listened to music just to escape my own thoughts.

Sometimes, out of nowhere, sleep would pull me back into it:

Scenes of the shooting happening all over again,
just in different places —
church, school, anywhere.

They aren't constant anymore,
but sometimes those nightmares still show up.

———

## GOING HOME

After three long months,
they finally prepared me to go home.

But home wasn't set up for a wheelchair.

• Doors weren't wide enough
• The bathroom wasn't accessible
• I had to transfer into a rolling computer chair just to get
through doorways and shower

Eventually, a ramp was built so I could enter the house.

41

That first night home…
it wasn't magical.

The routine was overwhelming.

Twice a day, I needed blood thinner shots in my stomach.

My mom tried so hard to hold it together.

But that first night, she broke.
She cried because it was a lot.

And when I saw her cry, I cried too.

I felt like a burden.
I felt like my injury had ruined everything.

We ended up holding each other,
both of us crying,
both of us exhausted,
both of us scared.

But we promised each other:

"We're going to get through this… Together."

# CHAPTER 7

---

## THE COURTROOM

Walking into that courtroom felt like walking back into the
night everything changed.

They called me to the stand, and suddenly I wasn't the victim
—
I was the one being interrogated.

The questions came fast, sharp.
My voice shook.

My hands trembled on the microphone.
I cried in front of a room full of strangers who had no idea
what it felt like to survive what I survived.

Then they brought him in.

The man who pulled the trigger.

He smiled.

Not a nervous smile.
Not a remorseful one.

A bold, careless smirk — like none of this was real, like I wasn't sitting there in a wheelchair because of him.

When he spoke to the judge, he said he wasn't a criminal.

Said he "didn't mean to hurt anyone."
Like those words could erase the damage.

I had written a letter, and I had to read it out loud — even though my whole body was shaking.

And I told him what his actions cost me —
the pieces of my life I can never get back.

Dance.
My ability to walk.
My job.
My independence.
The version of me I'll never meet again.

Every word felt like reopening a wound.

He showed nothing.

No regret.
No emotion.
Not even a flicker of understanding.

But the judge still sentenced him.

The judge gave him a sentence he couldn't smile his way through.

Justice didn't heal me.
It didn't bring back what I lost.

But standing there, trembling and still speaking my truth, taught me something:

He broke my body — but not my voice.
And not my strength.

# CHAPTER 8

---

## HIGH SCHOOL, PROM, AND FINDING MY BALANCE

It was time to go back to school.
When my dad told me I was going back, I was so against it.

I didn't want to be at school in a wheelchair.
I didn't want the stares, the questions, the sympathy.
I wanted to be home schooled, tucked away from people,
hidden from the world and everything I didn't feel ready to
face.

But he told me, "No. You're going back."

At the time, those words frustrated me.
I didn't feel strong.
I didn't feel brave.
I didn't feel like the girl who could show up in front of
everybody after surviving something I could barely talk about.

Looking back now, I'm so grateful that he pushed me.

———

The first day, walking — or rolling — into Everett High School, I felt the wheels of my wheelchair squeak against the linoleum floor. That sound felt louder than everything else. My heart raced, my palms were sweaty, and I prayed no one was staring—even though I knew everyone would be.

I felt like I was entering a world that used to be mine but didn't quite fit me anymore.

But when I arrived, everyone came around me, forming a big circle.

They showed me love, support, and inclusion.
It was overwhelming in the best way.

They weren't looking at the wheelchair.
They were looking at me.

The teachers, principals, and school nurse were amazing.
They made me feel supported, seen and valued.

———

Of course, there were moments I felt deeply isolated.

I lost some friends along the way — not because of them, but because I withdrew.

I didn't feel like myself, and I didn't know how to be around people while carrying everything I'd been through.

47

I remember Senior Skip Day, when we were planning to go to the movies all together. My friends said, "Well, who's going to sit with her?" The accessible seating was in the front row, and everybody wanted to sit in the back. I remember feeling isolated, hurt, and betrayed, so I didn't go. These were friends I had been close to, and in that moment, it felt like my disability had created a distance I couldn't bridge.

It wasn't just missing a movie.
It was missing the version of my life where I didn't have to think about accessibility or feel like an afterthought.

———

But through it all, I had people around me who cared and made an effort to include me. Those small efforts meant everything.

———

Slowly, as the days turned into months, I began learning how to juggle everything.

Balancing school, physical therapy, counseling, and work was exhausting, but with each small victory, I found my rhythm and a sense of control over my life again.

I worked at Younkers Department store while also working in a medical office as an office assistant—two jobs while still trying to graduate and recover.

On my 18th birthday, during my senior year, I moved into my

first apartment.
It wasn't perfect, but it was mine.
I was learning independence one day at a time.

————

Prom was a milestone I will never forget.

I wore a sky-blue, puffy dress that made
me feel like a princess.

My classmates surprised me
by surrounding me
and singing Ed Sheeran's *"Thinking Out Loud"*,
making me feel celebrated
and loved.

That moment captured the beauty of being supported and
included,
even after everything I had been through.
I realized that life's toughest battles could be softened by the
kindness of others, and that celebrating small victories
mattered just as much as surviving the hardships.

————

Through all of this — school, work, therapy, social events —
I was learning how to balance life again.

I didn't always succeed.

There were days I wanted to quit counseling and take
shortcuts in therapy.

Days where everything felt too heavy, too tiring, too unfair.
But each step, each struggle, shaped who I am today.

I learned resilience, patience,
and the importance of letting others in.

———

These experiences taught me that life isn't just about what
happens to you — it's about how you rise from it,
how you find your own strength,
and how you embrace the people who love you through every
version of you.

## JOURNAL ENTRY —
## "Buried, Then Born Again"
## (2017)

DATE: 2016

Sitting here overthinking, Driving myself insane.
Losing myself more and more each
day, Getting buried in this pain.
One tiny bullet that took away all the feeling.
Screaming out for help, Asking God for healing.
They say, don't stress over things you cannot change,
But more and more each day I began to become deranged.
Feeling alone and depressed. With no one to confide upon.
Killing the mind with thoughts of how the night should have gone.
I should have done this. I could have done that.
All my dreams and plans Now come to a halt and fall flat.
Life is now different — I never saw this coming.
The nerves corrupted. The body numbing.
A coward plus a gun. That leaves me stripped bare.
Robbed and condemned. Tied down to this chair.

— (Later addition) —

But my life ain't over.
Would you look at me?
I went through the storm and came out —
Now that's my testimony.
No, my life ain't perfect.
No it ain't quite sweet.
But I picked myself up and kept going,
Because I would never taste defeat.

# CHAPTER 9

---

# LOOK AT ME NOW

Today, she is not just surviving. She is living.

Every prayer whispered at sixteen—lying in a hospital bed, connected to tubes and uncertainty—has unfolded into reality. Peace, purpose, and a meaningful life are no longer distant hopes; they are real, tangible, and taking place.


Becoming the brand ambassador for the largest exoskeleton company is proof of that reality. Traveling with the company, walking alongside others, climbing flights of stairs—being paid to do what once seemed impossible—is a daily reminder of resilience and purpose.


She is also pursuing her business degree and has started multiple small businesses of her own, building the foundation for her dreams while inspiring others along the way.


In addition, she has begun motivational speaking at events and has returned to hospitals to talk to children in similar situations—showing them that life can still be full, beautiful, and meaningful, even after trauma.

If speaking to her sixteen-year-old self—the girl trapped in her own body, terrified, angry, unsure if life would ever be good again—she would gently hold her face and whisper: "Hold on. The life you're praying for is already waiting for you. You're going to live it."

She would be hugged so tight and told that laughter will return. Told that joy will return. Walking will return. Inspiring others all around the world will come true.

One day she wouldn't just survive this—she would become unstoppable because of it.

She's a business owner, entrepreneur, speaker, walker, dreamer, fighter.

Best of all, she is living in the prayers that once felt impossible. Every achievement, every step—literally and emotionally—is proof that pain has purpose, that broken things can become beautiful, that God heard every cry, even when it didn't feel like it.

The girl who once feared she would never walk again now embraces each step, assisted or not, strong, fearless, and unapologetically herself—an invincible being, unshaken by life's storms and unstoppable in her purpose.

***JOURNAL ENTRY — Look At Me (Age 17)***

## LOOK AT ME

I should be down and depressed,
but yet I'm still in a happy place.
I went through the worst of the worst
& still managed to put a smile on my face.

Look at me—physically held down,
but mentally standing tall
Triumphant through the bad,
though he wished that I would fall.

Look at me—an innocent bystander
with a bullet through my back,
still giving God the glory
even when my faith is under attack.

Look at me—remaining optimistic when my mind begins to wonder,
Making it through the storm:

-The rain.
-The sleet.
-The thunder.

## JOURNAL ENTRY — Look At Me (Continued…)

DATE: 2016

LOOK AT ME
And I mean, look at me good.
I am not an ordinary girl
that can easily be understood.
But would you look at me?

Continuing on with life
because I am tired of stressing.
The God I serve makes no mistakes.
And with time, there will come a blessing.

LOOK AT ME

# About the Author

Dalasia Jackson is a speaker, advocate, and entrepreneur whose journey of survival and resilience has inspired audiences across the country. After surviving a life-changing trauma at sixteen, she transformed her story into purpose — using her voice to bring hope to others facing their own battles.

Dalasia has worked alongside leading mobility-technology companies, shared her message at schools, hospitals, and community events, and continues to empower individuals to believe in healing, possibility, and strength beyond circumstance.

She is committed to reminding others that even in the hardest moments, life can still become meaningful, beautiful, and full of purpose.